Bush Babies

Roger & Pat de la Harpe
Nigel & Wendy Dennis

Bush Babies

Few experiences in life can match those of observing wildlife in its natural environment, and even fewer can match the enchanting sight of the birth of a new generation of animals, as they tentatively take their first steps into a brand new world.

Most females of the cat species wander off alone to choose a secluded and isolated location in which to give birth to their young. The cubs, blind, helpless and vulnerable to predation, are relocated by their leopard, cheetah and smaller cat mothers every few days to reduce the threat of danger to their offspring.

Not so for the lioness, however, who leaves the pride, sometimes accompanied by another female, and chooses a shady thicket of long grass, shrubs or a clump of reeds as her birthing place. Having a 'babysitter' enables the lioness to hunt, secure in the knowledge that her cubs are protected. The lioness will return to the pride with her cubs when they are between four and eight weeks old, but only if there are no other cubs in the pride that are younger than three months old. This is to prevent unnecessary competition for the still-suckling newcomers.

Although it is classed as a 'big' cat, the cheetah is timid by nature, and a mother rarely relaxes, keeping a constant lookout for any threat to her family.

A lioness and her young cubs, not yet part of the pride structure, cross a dry riverbed in search of shelter from the blazing sun.

Buffalo calves are usually born in the summer months, when the grass is most nutritious. Both mother and calf are particularly vulnerable at this time, and because of this the female does not move off to give birth, but rather stays with the herd for protection.

While lion cubs and lionesses are fortunate in that they join an extended family, leopard and cheetah mothers single-handedly raise their young.

Cat cubs, curious and playful, if somewhat a little unsteady on their feet, explore their new surroundings, and a reed, a branch or a stone becomes an object of play. And there is one thing no cub can resist – its mother's flicking tail. This moving 'oddity' becomes the target of their attentions: they stalk it, pounce on it and wrestle with it, their sharp little teeth sometimes causing their mother untold irritation. Lions are incredibly tolerant of the antics of young cubs, as they clamber all over them, try to trip them up and bite their ears and legs; they will, when necessary, however, discipline the youngsters with an intimidating snarl and a gentle cuff of a huge paw. Because of the pride situation, lion cubs have a host of playmates, but, like all babies, when the rough and tumble becomes too strenuous for them they return, chastened and subdued, to their mothers for comfort.

Elephant calves too are part of a herd structure, and are fiercely protected by the older animals. The cow, attended by other females, moves a short distance away from the herd to give birth and, at least for the first year, the elephant calf sticks close to its mother, seeking shelter

under her belly. It is always entertaining to watch a baby elephant trying to cope with its trunk. For the first six months of its life, it constantly trips over this strange appendage that swings uncontrollably from side to side as it tries to run. And when the calf tries to mimic the bulls

For the first two years of an elephant calf's life, it is very well protected by its mother, aunts and siblings, and is seldom, if ever, allowed to wander out of their sight.

Through the process of feather-wetting, the male sandgrouse is able to carry water over a long distance to his chicks and nest, often situated far away from the nearest watering point.

Brants' whistling rat babies hang onto tufts of hair on their mother's back as she scurries along, dragging them with her from burrow to burrow.

Darker in coloration than adults, even young aardwolves have the dark muzzle characteristic of this species.

and cows by using its trunk to draw up water, its seemingly unmanageable trunk flops all over the place, and the youngster spills more water than it gets to drink. Elephant calves take great delight in showing off their strength, and you will often see them chasing other animals – especially antelope species – from 'their' watering place. It is not even beyond them to chase after hapless ostriches, lumbering after these earth-bound birds as they run away with their wings outspread.

While the larger antelopes such as springbok, impalas, gemsbok and eland also form herd structures, the smaller species – specifically grysbok, duikers and steenbok – form family units consisting of parents and their single offspring. Lambs are born throughout the year, though certain species choose lambing seasons to coincide with a region's heavy rainfall and resulting abundance of grass.

Impalas and springbok give birth within a brief window of time during mid- to late summer. This mass breeding ensures that a large number of lambs will survive the heavy predation by lions, cheetahs, leopards, wild dogs and jackals. Females often hide their lambs in clumps of grass or bushes, returning to suckle and groom them twice a day. The period before introduction to either the herd or the family unit varies from species to species. Impala lambs join the herd after two days, while oribi lambs will stay hidden for four months.

Springbok, tsessebe, blesbok and impalas form 'nursery herds' within the main herd, and here lambs are anxiously watched over by their mothers.

Wildebeest calves are not as fortunate. In fact, wildebeest young have to learn to run almost as soon as they can stand. However, even within these species, where life is a frantic race to escape death, there is still a sense of playfulness, and calves will often kick up their heels out of sheer exuberance.

Springbok lambs are intensely curious, and have been seen to follow sandgrouses to see what the birds are about. One particular springbok lamb, nose to the ground right behind a sandgrouse at a watering point in the Kalahari, was so startled when the bird suddenly flew off that it ran a short distance before starting to 'pronk'. While the rest of the herd watched in amusement, the youngster did it over and over again, and soon all the lambs joined in – to the obvious displeasure of the thirsty birds.

If it's entertainment you are after, none of wildlife's young can match the primates. Mothers are devoted to, and protective of, their offspring, and will defend them at any cost. A new arrival is the centre of much curiosity, and it is not uncommon for the rest of the troop (with the

Ever watchful and alert, adult meerkats keep an eye on a youngster even while sunning themselves at the entrance to their burrow on a chilly winter's morning.

exception of the dominant males) to make a fuss of the baby. With no fixed breeding season, playmates abound – and play, they do. They chase one another up and down trees and over boulders, wrestling and tussling incessantly, and when that fall or bite is just a little too painful, scurry back to the comforting arms of their mothers for some tender loving care. Although primate young are allowed a lot of leeway, they are strictly disciplined. It is not uncommon for a young baboon throwing a 'tantrum', to be picked up and bitten on the foot by an older baboon. If it continues to scream, the adult will calmly repeat the punishment until the baby finally gets the message.

What we tend to forget is that the playful actions of animal babies are not done simply in the spirit of fun. The stalking, pouncing and wrestling that cubs do is all in training for the future, when they will need to hunt for themselves. The tiresome trunk that the elephant calf has to master will be used to feed on the topmost leaves of trees, and for 'digging' for water in times of drought. The 'pronking' actions of the springbok will later serve to show dominance during breeding, and to distract and evade predators. The primate's agility will ensure a hasty retreat up a cliff face or to a tree top, while its speed and strength are needed to outwit an attacker. What we perceive to be 'cute' and 'fun' is to these animals the basis of the hardest lesson in life – survival.

The diet of the bat-eared fox cub – found in semi-desert or open grasslands – consists mainly of insects.

Warthog piglets are born in a burrow, emerging after about two weeks to survey their new world.

Bat-eared fox cubs will not venture far from their den, and their acute sense of hearing will alert them to impending danger. Like all young animals, they are playful, and even a simple greeting between two siblings can lead to a bout of playfighting.

Bat-eared foxes are very protective of their young and, should disturbances occur at the den, will move them to a new one. To strengthen the bond between the mother and her offspring, they engage in sessions of mutual grooming.

Born blind, bat-eared fox cubs gain their eyesight after about nine days and will leave the burrow for short periods when they are between two and three weeks old. Weaned at about four weeks, cubs are fed by both parents at the den until they are old enough to accompany the adults on foraging expeditions. Bat-eared fox pairs stay together for many years – some say for life – and seldom move away from the territory they have chosen as their home range. As a result, some of their burrows are regularly reused during the pair's breeding lives.

Affectionate and demonstrative, meerkats spend a great deal of time grooming and cuddling one another while soaking up the sun outside their burrows. As the alpha male and female are generally the only breeding pair, one member of the group will act as a babysitter for the offspring while the rest go foraging for food. Naturally inquisitive, meerkats sit on their hind legs, all the better to view the passing parade, and will bolt for the nearest burrow at the first hint of danger. The youngsters indulge in a lot of playfighting, always under the watchful eye of an older meerkat. Meerkats remain in constant communication with the rest of the troop. Their wide repertoire of sounds ranges from a repeated, harsh barking that signifies danger or anger, to a gentle churring to keep track of youngsters during foraging expeditions.

While most of the larger antelope species hide their young immediately after birth, the length of time during which the calves stay hidden varies from species to species. Waterbuck calves (above) join the herd after three to four weeks, but the red hartebeest calf (opposite) will join its mother in the harem herd after only a few days.

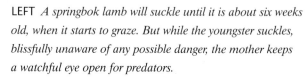

LEFT *A springbok lamb will suckle until it is about six weeks old, when it starts to graze. But while the youngster suckles, blissfully unaware of any possible danger, the mother keeps a watchful eye open for predators.*

BELOW *Eager to experiment with its newfound freedom, this very young lamb, with its spindly legs, attempts to imitate its elders. Its mother is, however, always in close attendance.*

OPPOSITE *Impala young interact constantly, resting and playing together. Mutual grooming around the neck and face, using the incisors to scrape the skin clean, is a popular pastime, and each lamb has a turn to groom and be groomed.*

ABOVE *Usually shy and retiring, the dainty bushbuck lamb stays close to watercourses and prefers the thick cover of dense vegetation for safety.*

BELOW *Zebra families usually consist of a stallion, two to six mares and their various offspring. Foals can stand within 15 minutes of birth, and suckle within the hour.*

OPPOSITE *A perfect imitation of its mother, this Burchell's zebra foal will be protected by the rest of the herd should danger threaten.*

ABOVE *Within minutes of birth, the blue wildebeest calf is capable of both standing and running. Wildebeest are particularly susceptible to predation in certain regions, and, because of this, being able to keep up with the herd is an imperative survival strategy.*
BELOW *The gemsbok female generally leaves the herd to give birth to her single, reddish-brown offspring, and will keep the calf well hidden for the first six weeks of its life.*

ABOVE *To protect her newborn calf, an nyala mother hides it in deep cover for the first two weeks of its life. Tentative by nature, nyalas are especially cautious at open water holes.*

BELOW *While female waterbuck calves are allowed to remain with the herd, males are chased away when they are about a year old, and join bachelor herds consisting of young males ousted from other breeding herds.*

The giraffe calf has the longest drop of all animals, as its mother gives birth standing upright. While this fall snaps the umbilical cord, it takes a while before the cord (above) drops off altogether. The mother will often leave her calf hidden while she feeds at distances of up to three kilometres away. Hidden calves lie down and will lay their necks flat on the ground should there be any threat of danger. This, however, makes them vulnerable to predation, particularly by lions.

ABOVE *Lion cubs are introduced to the pride when they are four to eight weeks old, and stay close to their mothers for about two years.*
BELOW *Lions are Africa's most sociable cat and, during the heat of the day, spend hours lolling around in the shade together. Cubs stay close to the pride for protection, the family group providing security for their playful young.*
OPPOSITE *Weary from playing, this youngster takes a break on a termite mound, although remaining alert to the possibility of being pounced on by a sibling.*

ABOVE *Lions, both male and female, are surprisingly tolerant of their offspring's exuberant antics and appear to be happy to endure being tugged, pulled and trampled on by their young.*

BELOW *Like parents everywhere, however, adult lions grab every opportunity for some peace and quiet, especially when their cubs have worn themselves out after hours of enthusiastic play.*

The spots on a lion cub's coat disappear as it grows older.

ABOVE Ever playful and bursting with energy, even siesta time becomes just another excuse for a bit of rough and tumble.

BELOW Weaned cubs and adults drink regularly when water is available, especially after feeding. Most of their moisture needs are, however, obtained from the blood of their prey.

ABOVE *Lion cubs are avid explorers and this fallen tree trunk provides a perfect vantage point from which to scan the veld.*

BELOW *Only about 10 weeks old and still vulnerable to predation, these youngsters remain close to thick cover for protection while their mother is away hunting.*

OPPOSITE *When times are hard and adults are forced to cover long distances in search of food, cub fatalities are high; the cubs die of starvation or abandonment and predation.*

OVERLEAF *Servals are mainly nocturnal animals, favouring areas where there is a high rainfall. During the day they hide up in thickets, reedbeds or long grass close to water.*

Largely solitary, servals are agile hunters, living on rodents, birds, insects, reptiles and even small antelope. They use their large ears to listen for any movement in the grass or reeds, and usually pounce on their prey, stunning it. This method is particularly successful when hunting rodents, but it is not their only tactic and servals are not averse to wading into water to catch frogs, fish or water birds.

ABOVE *A rare sight, the king cheetah cub's markings differ substantially from the common cheetah, with bolder black stripes and blotches on its back, although it retains the characteristic 'tear lines' on its face.*

BELOW *Alert to danger, this cheetah mother carefully checks the surrounding veld before moving her young cubs across open ground in search of a new hiding place.*

OPPOSITE *The bond between a cheetah mother and her offspring is particularly strong and she happily allows her cubs to clamber all over her, cuffing her with their paws and biting her face and tail.*

Cheetah cubs do not have an inherent ability to hunt, and up until the age of three months stay behind while their mother goes off in search of food. The mother 'instructs' them to hide with a certain call, and summons them with another, once she has killed. As they grow older, the cubs slowly start to follow their mother, often spoiling a chase as they play or run ahead. They only become successful hunters at about 15 months of age.

ABOVE LEFT *A baboon mother is a doting parent and makes soothing, clicking sounds to her infant as it suckles. At first, as the mother moves around, her offspring hangs onto her chest, but at about six months it begins to ride jockey-style.*
ABOVE RIGHT *Agile and quick, the baboon is able to climb any tree and learns from the example of others which fruits are edible.*
BELOW *With no fixed breeding season, a newcomer to the baboon troop never lacks for playmates of all ages.*
OPPOSITE *These two young baboons caused such absolute mayhem within the troop that they were seemingly well and truly disciplined – hence their contrite expressions.*

ABOVE *Chimpanzees spend a lot of time in trees, both when feeding and when seeking safety,*
and this young chimp will soon become as adept at climbing as its mother.
BELOW *Vervet monkeys spend many hours grooming one another, at the same time making*
contented chattering sounds. Mutual grooming reinforces social bonds between troop members.
OPPOSITE *The bond between a mother chimpanzee and her baby is intensely strong, and the*
mother chimp will defend her offspring even at the cost of her own life.

ABOVE *Hyena cubs are particularly precocious, and sibling rivalry between cubs of the same sex is common. Year-old cubs are weaned over several months, and, much to the mother's irritation, are prone to petulant behaviour at this time.*

BELOW *A hyena cub extracts regurgitated meat from its mother's mouth after she has returned from a hunt. The spotted hyena makes its characteristic 'whooping' calls when it is out foraging for food, and its 'laughing' sounds when it competes for its share at a kill.*

OPPOSITE *Hyena cubs start following their mothers on hunting expeditions when only a few months old, but will not take part in an actual hunt until they are nearly fully grown. Males reach sexual maturity at two years, and females at three.*

The female Nile crocodile is alerted to the fact that her young are ready to hatch when, after a period of some 84 days, she hears squawking sounds coming from her nest buried beneath the sand. She scrapes the soil away to uncover as many as 80 eggs, and the hatchlings emerge, squirming and squealing. She gathers them up into her mouth and carries them to the water, where she opens her jaws below the surface, and releases them. Once in the nursery area, the young continue making high-pitched calls to stay in contact with each other and their mother. At this time they eat aquatic insects, small frogs and crabs and keep close to reeds and overhanging vegetation, which offer protection against predators. After about six weeks, they disperse and leave the nursery area.

The loggerhead turtle returns to the same beach to nest, year after year, from October to February. The female emerges from the sea at night and digs her nest above the high-water mark, laying about 120 eggs at a time. The incubation temperature of the eggs determines the sex of her offspring: an approximate 24°C will ensure male births, and 29°C female. After a period of about 70 days, the hatchlings emerge at night, and begin their journey to the sea, many falling prey to ghost crabs, birds and even jackals.

ABOVE *Leopard cubs have an inherent ability to hunt, and will accompany their mothers on such an excursion when they are just over nine months. By 11 months, they are sufficiently skilled to make their own kill of an impala or similar-sized antelope.*
OPPOSITE *A young leopard plays constantly and is particularly fond of climbing trees and leaping and tumbling in the grass. These activities hone its skills for the time when, at the age of about 18 months, it leaves its mother to fend for itself.*

Elephant cows can conceive for the first time once they have reached the age of nine years. After a gestation period of 22 months, a single calf is born, although twins are not that uncommon. For the first two years of its life, the calf will stay close to its mother within the herd, and she will help it across rough terrain and over obstacles, and generally keep it as safe as possible from danger.

Elephant calves have poor eyesight, and stay in contact with their mothers by 'feeling' with their trunks. A very young calf will seek shelter under its mother's belly, and will stay there when the herd moves, always at the pace of the slowest member of the group. A calf will suckle for between two and three years, depending on climatic conditions, but under normal circumstances will be weaned by the age of two years. In this matriarchal society, young bulls leave the family group when they reach puberty, linking up with other lone males. Bulls will only return to their family groups to mate. Although old bulls tend to be solitary, they will sometimes have an escort of younger bulls, which not only serve to protect their older counterparts, but also learn from them.

It will take about six months before an elephant calf learns to control the strange appendage – it's trunk – that is so vital to its existence. Calves are very playful and take great delight in pushing one another around. While the older calves often bully the younger ones, they may well be disciplined by the females with a swift smack of the trunk if they go too far.

TOP *This ungainly immature blackcrowned night heron does not resemble its handsome parent in any way, but it quickly loses its bittern-like appearance as it moults into adult plumage.*
ABOVE *The female jacana is larger than the male, and she will mate, lay her eggs and then move on to a new partner, leaving the male to incubate and tend the eggs, and raise the young.*
RIGHT *Egyptian geese are notorious for choosing strange places to nest, but will always lead their chicks to water, be it a stream or a dam. The goslings are able to swim within 24 hours of hatching, and are also fully capable of fending for themselves.*

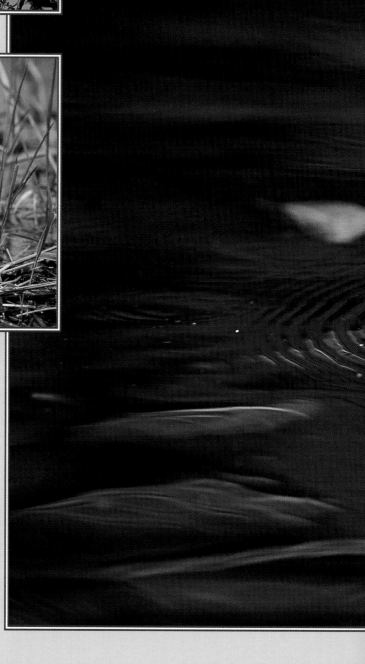

Newborn black-backed jackals are grey-brown in colour, and lack the distinctive markings of the adults. They are born in old aardvark holes or other disused burrows, but from the age of about three months, they usually sleep above ground under bushes. The pups are looked after by both parents as well as by their older siblings, which assist in feeding, teaching and grooming. As they grow, they become increasingly adventurous and begin to forage for food, and by six months the jackal pups are reasonably efficient hunters.

ABOVE *Wild dog pups stay in the den and will only emerge when there are babysitters in close attendance. At birth, they are black and white, and they will only start developing the distinctive adult coloration as they age.*

BELOW *Most wild dog pups are born in the dry, winter months, when hunting conditions are optimal, enabling the adults to operate closer to the den. A pack may return to the same area to den, or even to the same den, year after year.*

OPPOSITE *Left behind at the burrow, the pups eagerly await the return of the pack from a hunt. When the adults arrive back at the den, they are besieged by the hungry pups, squealing in delight and demanding their share of the meat that is regurgitated for them.*

THESE PAGES *The solitary and elegant Cape fox feeds on insects,
spiders, reptiles and mice, as well as wild fruits and berries. A
quick sniff and a tentative nip will soon teach this youngster that
millipedes are unpalatable. Females give birth to between two and
five pups in a disused aardvark burrow, and will stay with the pups
until they are old enough to disperse and live on their own. Cape
foxes are mainly nocturnal, and, during daylight hours, prefer to
stay under dense cover of bush, or in burrows – which they dig
themselves – to prevent detection by predators.*

OVERLEAF *This suckling white rhino calf, weighing 40 kilograms
at birth, is dependent on its mother for about a year, during which
time she is fiercely protective of it. Calves can stand within an hour
of birth, and begin grazing at two months.*

SUNBIRD
PUBLISHING

First published 2002
2 4 6 8 10 9 7 5 3 1

Sunbird Publishing (Pty) Ltd
34 Sunset Avenue, Llandudno, Cape Town, South Africa
Registration number: 4850177827

Publisher Dick Wilkins
Editor Brenda Brickman
Designer Mandy McKay
Production Manager Andrew de Kock

Reproduction by Unifoto (Pty) Ltd, Cape Town
Printed and bound by Tien Wah Press (Pte) Ltd, Singapore

ISBN 0 624 04099 2